N | 1 | 0

W | 2

# Picture History of the 20th Century

## of the

## 20th Century

# THE 1940s

## Tim Wood and R.J. Unstead

FRANKLIN WATTS
LONDON•SYDNEY

This book has been produced from notes written by R. J. Unstead, the leading author of history books for children, before his death in 1988.

This edition © 2004 Franklin Watts

Franklin Watts
96 Leonard Street
London
EC2A 4XD

Franklin Watts Australia
45-51 Huntley Street
Alexandria
NSW 2015

ISBN 0 7496 5668 9

First published in 1991

Design: K and Co
Editor: Hazel Poole
Picture Research: Jan Croot
                    Sarah Ridley

Printed in Belgium

A CIP catalogue record for this book is available from the British Library

# Contents

# Introduction

The decade of the 1940s is dominated by the Second World War. Until 1945 the world was engaged in the most costly and destructive war in history affecting everybody in various ways. For many people the war years were a desperate struggle for survival as many homes, cities and lives were lost.

Before 1942 it seemed as if victory was impossible. However, when Hitler invaded Russia and later declared war on the United States after the Japanese attack on Pearl Harbor, he over-reached himself. After that, although it was not obvious at the time, his defeat was inevitable and Germany finally surrendered in May 1945, bringing six years of fighting, devastation and loss to an end.

Perhaps the most dramatic result of the war was the sudden confrontation in Europe between the Soviet Union and the United States which changed the face of world politics. Stalin, the "gallant Russian ally" was suddenly seen as a bloody-handed tyrant.

In an astonishing reversal yesterday's enemies were helped to their feet and given the aid they needed to rebuild their countries and regain their places in a world which was now dominated by two "super-powers".

The second half of the decade saw a surprisingly rapid post-war recovery. There had been rapid advances in science, technology and medical knowledge largely the by-products of wartime research and development which now had peacetime applications.

Peace also brought social change as the war undermined old attitudes and replaced them with a new spirit of community. The success of the United Nations organisation in dealing with post-war problems such as refugees and food shortages seemed to offer hope for future international co-operation.

# The nature of World War II

In many ways, the Second World War was a continuation of the First, fought by almost the same contestants and for many of the same reasons.

However, it was much more widespread than before and almost every corner of the world was touched in some way by the fighting and its effects. It also proved to be a great deal more destructive and immensely more cruel than any previous war.

The use of aeroplanes in support of tanks made it mainly a war of movement. In 1940, the Germans used *blitzkrieg* or "lightning war" to overrun and occupy most of Western Europe with astonishing ease.

While Russia, the United States and Britain led the bitter five year struggle to free the occupied countries from Nazi control, millions of Eastern Europeans were used by the Nazis as slave labour. Millions of others were put into concentration camps. Probably one quarter of the population of Europe was displaced by the war, either forcibly or as they fled from the enemy.

This was a total war, fought not just by soldiers, sailors and airmen, but also by civilian populations. The long range bombers which pounded factories and destroyed cities, also brought women and children into the front line of battle.

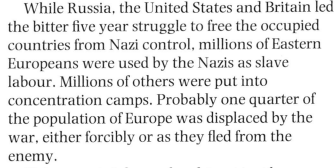

◁ Blitzkrieg! German tanks supported by Stuka dive bombers smashed through the badly equipped Allied armies during the first half of the war. Motorised infantry then rushed through the gaps to mop up the enemy's broken forces.

▽ Threatened by advancing armies and made homeless by the bombing of their cities, millions of people became refugees.

△ Major cities throughout Europe suffered as a result of enemy bombing. Here, amidst the ruins of Nuremberg, Hitler's surviving lieutenants were put on trial in November 1945, accused of crimes against humanity. It was the first trial of its kind and the world was horrified by the evidence of widespread Nazi atrocities.

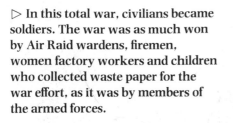

▷ In this total war, civilians became soldiers. The war was as much won by Air Raid wardens, firemen, women factory workers and children who collected waste paper for the war effort, as it was by members of the armed forces.

# Blitzkrieg!

The "phoney war" ended dramatically in May 1940, when Hitler's tanks burst through Holland and Belgium into France, throwing the Allies into total confusion.

The British army made a miraculous escape from Dunkirk and eight days later France surrendered to the enemy. In order to claim total victory the Nazis only had to win air supremacy while their forces crossed the Channel. However, in the Battle of Britain, the RAF destroyed so many German planes that Hitler cancelled the invasion and attacked the Soviet Union instead.

In December 1941 the Japanese, wanting to seize a rich empire in south-east Asia, tried to neutralize US naval power in the Pacific. Japanese aircraft made a surprise attack on the US Pacific Fleet. Eight American battleships and many other smaller ships were torpedoed or bombed. Luckily, the main US carrier force escaped the attack but this incident was to prove a turning point in the war.

△ On June 14 1940, the German army entered Paris.

◁ During the first few days of June 1940, the encircled British army was evacuated from Dunkirk. An armada of small fishing boats and pleasure craft sailed to France to help to rescue the stranded soldiers.

▽ RAF Mosquitos taking off at dawn to attack German shipping off the Norwegian coast. The bomber was the main strike weapon against Nazi-occupied Europe.

▷ On June 22 1941, Hitler's armies invaded Russia. They made huge advances at first but by December they had been brought to a standstill by General Zhukov and Russia's oldest ally, the winter snows.

▽ On December 7, 1941, without any warning, Japanese planes attacked the US naval base at Pearl Harbor, Hawaii. Within hours the United States, which had been neutral up to this point, declared war on Japan.

# The home front

During the war, whole populations had to be mobilised to help the war effort. Millions of men were conscripted into the armed forces. Women or retired people rushed to take over their jobs in the factories.

In Britain, shortages of food, clothes and fuel caused the introduction of rationing and the "Dig for Victory" campaign. The government organised Air Raid Precautions, war production and the distribution of food. Local Defence Volunteers were formed to guard against invasion. Everyone had their job to do.

Civilians also came into the front line in occupied Europe. Millions were used as forced labour or put into concentration camps. In many countries resistance movements were formed to undermine the German occupation.

It was a war that affected nearly everybody in some way.

△ At the outbreak of war, the British government feared that the bombing of large cities would cause millions of casualties. Arrangements were made to evacuate children from the towns to the safety of the countryside. Air Raid Precautions included a blackout of streets and houses, air raid sirens to warn of approaching bombers and extra emergency services.

◁ There were no deep shelters in London so many people spent the night in underground stations. Several stations were hit by bombs and at least 500 people were killed. However, this did not stop those Londoners who preferred the companionship of the stations to the lonely dampness of their garden shelters.

◁ The Ministry of Food told Britons how to eat wisely.

△ Local Defence Volunteers practise their shooting.

▷ "The Kitchen Front" – a poster advertising 122 wartime recipes which were broadcast on British radio by famous people. This was just one of the many ways in which the Ministry of Food told Britons how to make the best of their rations.

▽ Scrap metal was collected throughout the United States and Britain for the war effort.

# Women at war

In contrast to Germany where women were never fully mobilized, British women were conscripted into the services or into war work in 1942. Millions of men had left their jobs to join the armed forces. Women replaced them in every walk of life, including heavy and dangerous jobs, like working in shipyards and in munitions factories.

For many women their war work gave them a wage for the first time, though this did not necessarily compensate them for the long hours and boredom of much of the work. They also had to suffer a good deal of prejudice at first, although this largely died away when they more than proved their worth.

In addition to doing their war work, women also had to deal with the strains and problems of losing their husbands or men friends to the forces, or of losing their children to evacuation and also ran the risk of finding their homes bombed. After the Blitz it was women who had to feed, clothe and keep their families together. Women proved to be the greatest unused natural resource the country had.

△ Much of the dangerous work in munitions factories was done by women. Here a Merlin engine is being given a final inspection.

◁ The German U-boat campaign caused major food shortages in Britain. As young farm labourers joined the forces, thousands of women volunteered for the Land Army to work on the land. Many people were surprised that women could do heavy work like this.

◁ Women of the ATS operating searchlights. Women worked in every branch of the armed forces. They were nurses, radio operators and worked the rangefinders for anti-aircraft guns. Some flew planes, ferrying them from the factory to the air field. These were dangerous jobs, but only members of the Women's Home Defence Corps were trained to shoot.

▽ These members of the Women's Royal Naval Service (Wrens) are fitting smoke floats to a trainer aircraft of the Fleet Air Army. Women proved themselves not only to be the equal of men, but in many cases they were thought to be better at certain jobs, especially those involving delicate instruments or great concentration. Some died like men as well.

# Triumphs and disasters

Before 1942, the Allies had been defeated on all fronts. The Germans occupied Europe and much of Russia. The Japanese occupied much of Asia.

Then, quite suddenly it seemed, the tide turned. The German invasion of Russia faltered in the face of stubborn Russian resistance.

In North Africa, the British Eighth Army, led by General Montgomery, won a great victory at El Alamein. American forces landed in Tunisia and then, within a few months, 110,000 members of Rommel's Afrika Corps had been taken prisoner.

In July 1943, as a first step towards an invasion of Italy, Allied forces landed on the island of Sicily. Then the United States invaded Salerno and began to advance up the Italian peninsular.

Meanwhile, the Germans were badly defeated at Stalingrad. In Burma, Indian soldiers began to win victories against the Japanese. In Britain the churchbells, which had been the warning signal for a German invasion, were rung for the first time since the war began.

▽ A Japanese air raid on an Allied fuel dump "somewhere in the Pacific". Australian troops work desperately to roll fuel drums out of danger.

Japanese troops advancing into Burma (top). The capital, Rangoon, fell in March 1942 and main oilfields were destroyed to prevent them falling into Japanese hands.

△ On February 15 1942, the Japanese captured the great naval base and fortress of Singapore. It was believed to be impregnable. Its loss was a heavy blow to the Allies.

△ Russian soldiers
advancing through the
ruins of Stalingrad. The
German 6th Army reduced
the city to rubble but failed
to capture it. The Russians
hung on grimly, and in
November 1942,
surrounded and defeated
the Germans.

△ General Montgomery,
commander of the British
Eighth Army looks over El
Alamein.

▷ US tanks roll ashore
from landing craft during
the Allied landing at
Anzio, Italy, in May 1944.

# The war at sea

The war at sea lasted through the whole war. It was vital that the Allies won it because Britain could not survive without food and war materials which were brought from abroad by sea.

Although British shipping faced the threat of German surface raiders, like the *Graf Spee* and the *Bismarck*, the most serious danger came from beneath the waves – the German U-boat fleet. It was not until the later part of the war that the U-boats were overcome.

This was largely thanks to the convoy system, where a small number of warships could protect a large number of merchant ships. Fitting ships with radar and asdic underwater detection equipment also helped to defeat the U-boat menace.

In the Pacific, aircraft carriers fought a new kind of long range war where the ships involved were too far apart to see each other. American victories in the Coral Sea, off Midway Island and in the Leyte Gulf destroyed Japanese naval power.

This enabled US forces to "leapfrog" through the Pacific recapturing Japanese-held islands as they went.

▽ The German surface raider *Bismarck* fires at *HMS Hood*. A few minutes later *HMS Hood* was hit and exploded, with the loss of 1,418 lives.

The British navy then hunted down and sank the *Bismarck*. The sailors being picked up were blown off the *Bismarck's* decks during the battle.

◁ Officers of the Royal Navy and RAF Coastal Command in Operations Rooms on shore organizing the movement of ships and planes defending the waters of Britain. Their most vital role was the protection of homecoming convoys.

△ Sailors bombing up a Grumman Avenger on the deck of the aircraft carrier *HMS Indomitable*.

◁ A Japanese kamikaze pilot, his plane loaded with high explosives, trying to crash on to an American ship.

▽ Hellcat fighters on the deck of *HMS Indomitable* during the attack on Japanese-held oil refineries in Sumatra. The fighters escorted the bomber strike force on its mission but their main task was to defend the carrier from incoming enemy bombers.

# Towards victory

On D-Day, June 6 1944, ferried by a huge fleet of ships and protected by the largest airforce in the world, Allied forces landed on the coast of Normandy in northern France. The Germans, who had been expecting the invasion to come across the Channel near Calais, hesitated for a few vital days. During this period, the Allied troops successfully completed the largest sea-borne invasion in history and established a powerful bridgehead.

Six weeks later, reinforced by a steady stream of men and equipment, the Allies launched their attack towards Paris.

Caught between this formidable force approaching from the west and the advancing Russians in the east, the Germans fled for their own frontiers. One by one the countries of Europe were liberated. Once the Allies had crossed the Rhine, the Germans soon surrendered and the Nazi regime came to an end.

In the east, British and Commonwealth troops drove the Japanese out of Burma while the Americans reconquered the Philippines. The war ended soon after the dropping of two atomic bombs on Hiroshima and Nagasaki in August 1945, inflicting great devastation. Within a few weeks, Japan had surrendered.

On August 14 1945 the most costly and bloody war ever fought, finally came to an end and Europe was left to pick up the pieces.

△ French tanks being welcomed by civilians near Paris. Paris was liberated on 25 August 1944.

▽ American soldiers drag survivors ashore after their landing craft had sunk during the D-day landings.

▷ It was not until March 1945 that the Allies managed to cross the Rhine, Germany's formidable western border. The Germans were trapped between two overwhelming forces and their resistance finally crumbled. On April 25 1945, American soldiers advancing from the west met Russian soldiers advancing from the east on the banks of the River Elbe, south of Berlin. Five days later, trapped amidst the blazing ruins of his capital city in his underground bunker, and unable to face capture, Hitler committed suicide. On May 7, the German forces surrendered and the Nazi empire which Hitler had boasted would last for a thousand years, came to an end. The Allies could then turn their full energies towards victory against Japan.

△ American soldiers digging in on the beaches of Leyte Island. The United States reconquest of the Pacific islands put a stranglehold on Japan.

▽ The devastation of Hiroshima after the explosion of the atomic bomb. Many have criticised the dropping of the bomb, pointing out that Japan was already near collapse, her people starving and her industry ruined. Others have said that the final defeat of Japan would have cost millions of Allied lives.

# Cleaning up Europe

After the end of the war, enormous problems, social and economic, were brought to light. About 50 million people had been killed and large areas of Europe had been laid waste by the fighting. Millions of refugees needed to be resettled, fed and clothed. The United States' government put forward the Marshall Plan to help to pay for the recovery of Europe.

In Germany, a de-Nazification programme was put into operation. Non-Nazis were placed in important positions and Nazi leaders were tried for "war crimes".

As an added complication to this situation, the Soviet Union refused to give up the lands which she occupied in eastern Europe. The United States' government was not prepared to stand by while a large part of Europe became communist. So, in 1947, President Truman announced that the United States would resist any further extension of communism into Europe. The United States and the Soviet Union, the former war-time Allies, now found themselves in opposing camps.

△ Berlin, reduced to rubble by Allied bombing, was divided into four zones. The Western Allies created a democratic government in Germany to replace Nazi dictatorship and helped German industries to recover.

▽ The full horror of the Nazi regime was revealed when the concentration camps were opened up. These slave labourers at Buchenwald Camp survived. Millions of others, men, women and children did not.

△ Millions of Germans fled from the advancing Russians, preferring to surrender to the British, Americans or French. When the war ended and Germany was divided into four zones of occupation, many Germans refused to return to their homes in the Russian sector but were forced to do so by the Western Allies.

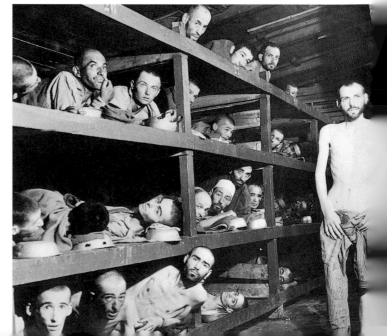

△ Berlin lay deep within the Russian zone. In 1948, Stalin tried to persuade Berliners to join the Soviet sector by blocking routes into the city. The Western Allies responded by airlifting in supplies.

▷ At the Yalta Conference in February 1945, the Allied leaders agreed how Germany would be smashed, divided and punished, and how Europe would be rehabilitated. However, this was the last time the war leaders met. Shortly afterwards, Churchill lost power in a general election and Roosevelt died. East-West relations soon worsened as Russia drew an "Iron Curtain" across the frontiers of the lands she occupied and refused to allow free elections to be held in Eastern Europe. The "Cold War" had begun.

# Post-war Britain

Britain ended the war tired, shabby and virtually bankrupt. At the general election in 1945, the Labour party swept to power. The British voters rejected Churchill, in spite of his brilliant wartime leadership. Part of the reason for this was that the Labour Party seemed to promise reform and a new approach to Britain's problems which was what the country wanted at that time.

The Labour government lost no time in introducing many of the measures recommended in the Beveridge Report of 1942, to destroy the "five evil giants" of want, ignorance, squalor, disease and unemployment. The core of their policy was the introduction of the Welfare State and the National Health Service. However, industrial recovery was a much slower process. There were many shortages and food, petrol, coal and even bread were rationed.

◁ People queueing for coal during the winter of 1947, which was one of the worst winters ever recorded in British history.

△ VE Day celebrations in London.
▽ Anxious women waiting for their returning husbands and sweethearts.

▷ The coal mines were nationalized in 1947. It was just one of a number of key industries dealt with in this way by the new Labour government elected in 1945. The spirit of equality built up during the war and the determination that the sacrifices of war should be worthwhile, inclined the voters towards Labour. It had been the "people's war" and now most looked for a people's peace. The Labour party offered a continuance of the kind of state intervention which people had grown to expect during the war years.

◁ The national milk scheme, introduced in 1940, continued after the war. This was a welcome extra benefit at a time when rationing had returned and there were shortages of food. These children could look forward to modern schooling under the 1944 Education Act. This gave free secondary education to all and created a three level system with primary schools, secondary schools and colleges of further education.

▷ A quick answer to the post-war housing shortage caused by the bombing of cities, was the prefabricated house. These were affectionately known as "prefabs". The government also began to build new towns like Stevenage, Welwyn Garden City, Peterlee and East Kilbride. People were moved to them from the inner city slums which were then cleared away.

# A changed world: the Far East

Japan surrendered shortly after atomic bombs were dropped on Hiroshima and Nagasaki by the United States' Air Force in August 1945. Japan was then occupied by American troops, given economic aid and educated to become a democracy.

The old colonies liberated from Japanese rule demanded independence. Although the French tried to hold on to Vietnam and the Dutch tried to retain the Dutch East Indies, it was to no avail as, along with the British, they found their empires melting away.

In China the corrupt Nationalist regime of Chiang Kai-Shek was swept away and replaced, in 1949, by the Communist People's Republic of China led by Mao Tse Tung.

△ Mao Tse Tung, leader of the Chinese communists. He created a peasant militia and taught them the principles of guerilla warfare which they used to fight the Japanese from 1937 to 1945.

◁ Indian machine gunners on Pagoda Hill during the battle of Fort Dufferin. The Japanese put up a fanatical, suicidal resistance before being overcome by the Fourteenth Army, led by General Sir William Slim.

▽ The British flag hoisted at Fort Dufferin in March 1945. The fort was one of the main Japanese strongholds in Mandalay. Its capture broke the Japanese forces and opened the gateway for the Allies to push towards Rangoon, the capital of Burma. The country became independent three years later.

◁ President Chiang Kai-Shek at a final parade just before he left the mainland in 1949 to set up Nationalist China on the island of Formosa.

▷ Ho Chi Minh (second from the left) the leader of the Vietnamese Communist Party was elected President of the Democratic Republic of Vietnam in December 1946. Within a few months he was leading an armed struggle for independence from the French.

# India and Israel

India played a vital part in the war, providing supplies and raising an army of two million men. However, in return for this the Congress demanded that India should become independent.

In 1947, Lord Mountbatten was appointed viceroy to oversee this process. Mountbatten decided to partition the country to satisfy the Muslims who wanted their own separate state of Pakistan.

As independence day approached in August 1947, Muslims fled from India and Hindus fled from Pakistan. In the confusion there were riots and massacres. Nearly half a million people were killed.

After their persecution under the Nazis, the Jews were determined to found their own national state. They chose Palestine, the biblical home of the Jews.

Since 1917 Palestine had been controlled by the British. As Jewish immigrants flooded in after 1945, the Arabs living there strongly objected. The British, who found themselves caught between Arab and Israeli guerilla forces, withdrew.

The declaration of the Jewish state of Israel on May 14 1948 led to Egyptian and Jordanian attacks which were repulsed by the Israelis.

By 1949, the Arabs and Israelis were living in uneasy peace.

◁ Mountbatten and Nehru, who became the first Prime Minister of India, holding discussions. Nehru wanted to make India into a powerful modern state. However, the world's largest democracy faced many economic and political problems.

▽ Tear gas being used against Muslim demonstrators in Lahore. One of the victims of these racial and religious tensions was Mahatma Gandhi, who was assassinated by a Hindu fanatic in 1948.

△ Jewish soldiers fighting Jordan's
crack Arab legion during the siege of
Jerusalem. There was heavy fighting
in the holy city, during which the
United Nations mediator was killed
by Israeli soldiers. However, the
30,000-strong Israeli army, the
Haganah, proved more than a match
for the Arabs. They not only repelled
the attacks but also advanced to
occupy Arab territory. Eventually a
truce was signed in 1949.

▷ Jewish immigrants arriving in
Israel. The Israeli victory in 1948 led
to a great increase in the number of
Jews immigrating to the new nation.
They set to work with great energy
and imagination to make the "desert
blossom". However, their arrival
underlined the fact that nearly a
million Palestinian Arabs were now
refugees from their former homes.
Their desire to return to their
homeland was to cause great
problems in the future.

# Science and technology

The need to win the war stimulated research and development in many scientific fields during the first half of the decade. Many of the discoveries concerned weapons, such as the development of rockets by the Germans and building of the first atomic bomb by the United States. However, some of this research had peacetime applications.

Work with radar and radio helped to develop new electronic equipment, such as transistors which were invented in 1947 and used in computers after the war. The development of the jet engine proceeded at a great pace. The sound barrier was broken in 1947 and the first commercial jet airliner, *The Comet*, flew in 1949.

In 1944, American Oswald Avery discovered that inherited characteristics were passed on through an acid called DNA which carried the genetic information needed by most living cells. Two years later events like these could be recorded with the first "Biro" ballpoint pens.

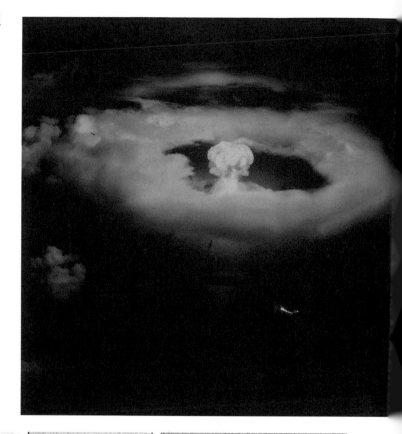

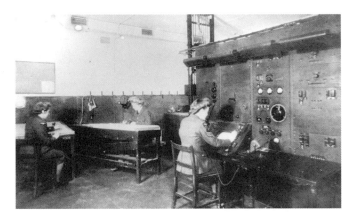

△ Radar, which came to be a key weapon, being used to detect approaching enemy bombers in the war.

▷ The ballpoint pen was invented by a Hungarian journalist, Laszlo Biro, in 1938. It first went on sale in November 1946.

◁ An American atomic bomb test at Bikini Atoll in the Pacific on July 1st, 1946.

◁ A magic eye camera gives a sequence of shots of the V-2 rocket. The rocket, used to attack Britain in 1945, flew at 6,080 kph (3,800 mph).

▷ The computer was developed shortly after the war. Known as "electronic brains", they were much bigger and slower than modern machines. Computers were used to calculate wages. The information is typed in code on to a tape which is then fed into the machine.

# Medicine

The war forced great advances in medicine and surgery. Since the Allied governments needed fit and healthy people for the war effort they were prepared to pay for research to be done into nutrition and preventitive medicine, such as immunisation.

In Britain, the Ministry of Food advised people on what to eat and how to make the best use of the scarce food they had. Soldiers were given synthetic vitamins and dehydrated food packs called K-rations to ensure they had a balanced diet.

The need to treat large numbers of wounded servicemen led to significant advances in blood transfusion services, plastic surgery, organ replacement and the use of antibiotics to prevent infection. These developments continued after the war and helped greatly to improve medical treatment throughout the remainder of the decade.

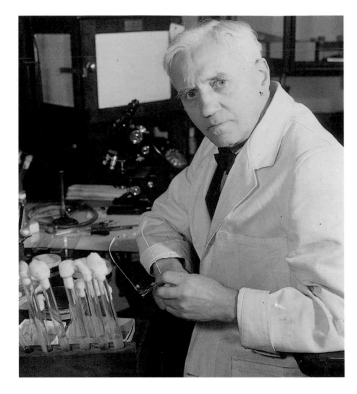

▽ A child being innoculated against diphtheria. Innoculation campaigns became common in the war and were continued afterwards. As a result certain diseases like diphtheria and malaria were virtually wiped out in Europe. This was an important step towards the idea that disease could be prevented rather than simply cured.

△ Sir Alexander Fleming, discoverer of the first antibiotic, penicillin. It was particularly useful for treating wounded soldiers. Other antibiotics like streptomycin and neomycin were discovered during the 1940s.

▽ WACs and enlisted men donating blood to the American Red Cross. During the war the American Red Cross organized a massive and efficient blood bank which saved many lives.

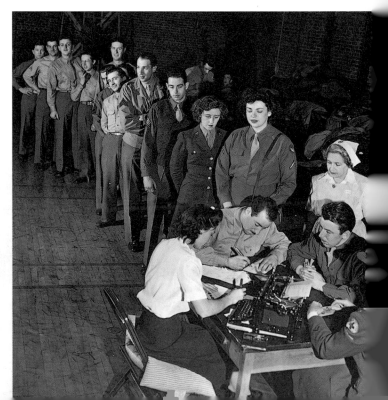

▷ Proper dental care was another aspect of preventitive medicine. After 1948, with the introduction of the National Health Service, dental treatment was free for all in Britain. Before this time dental treatment was a luxury which only the rich could afford and poorer people only went to the dentist to have a painful tooth extracted.

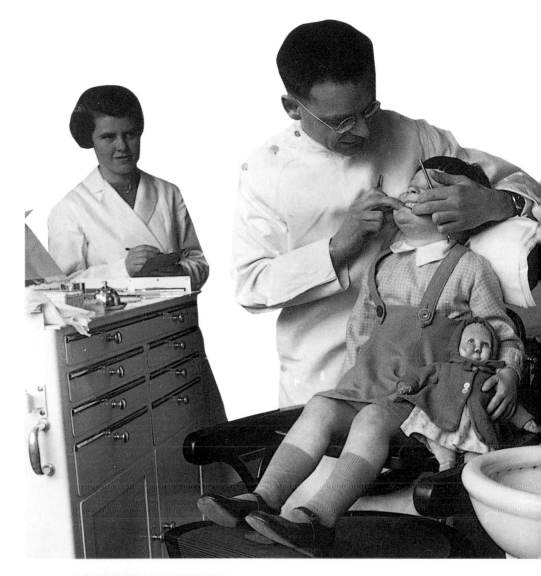

◁ Scientists are seen here working with vitamins. Food shortages during the war led to serious studies of nutrition and diet. As a result, although there was less food, people were better fed and healthier than ever before.

31

# Fashion

During the war, fashion reflected the need for practical garments suitable for war work. Men mainly wore uniforms. Women wore easy-fitting, plain clothes with square military shoulders.

With shortages of cloth, rationing was introduced and frivolity was frowned on. Decorative details like trouser turn-ups and pocket flaps disappeared and plain and practical outfits took their place. The government encouraged people to "make do and mend". It even became patriotic to have patches. At the end of the war, demobilized servicemen were given "demob" clothing at government clothing centres.

After the war women were delighted by a return to more elegant fashions when the French designer, Christian Dior, introduced his "New Look" in 1947, which brought back a more feminine shape to women's clothes.

COMFORT

UTILITY
WOVEN POPLIN Tunic Shirts. Attractive Stripe pattern. Collar attached.
RS300 BLUE STRIPE
RS301 GREY STRIPE
RS302 BROWN STRIPE
5 Coupons.                          Price 11/3

Sizes stocked:
14, 14½, 15,
15½, 16, 16½
ins.

UTILITY
SELF COLOUR
POPLIN Tunic
Collar

WHITE        8/7
BLUE         8/5
NUFF         8/5
upons

UTILITY
quality PRINTED POPLIN
shirts. Collar attached.
BLUE STRIPE
FAWN STRIPE
GREY STRIPE
ons                          Price 8/5

△ During the war people could buy plain "utility" clothing.

(Top) Olympia was used as a government clothing centre.

◁ Discharged airmen, wearing their "demob" suits, step cheerfully back to "civvy street".

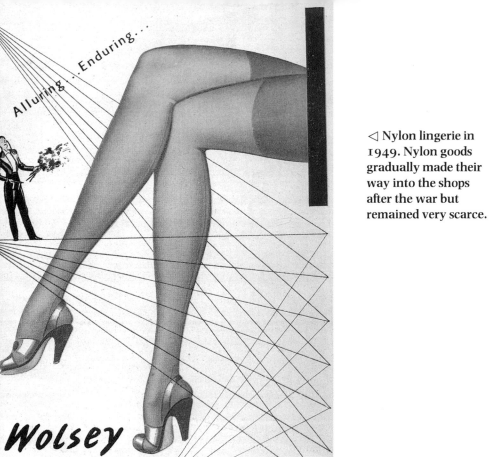

Alluring ...Enduring...

**Wolsey**

**nylons**

Wolsey Limited Leicester

◁ Nylon lingerie in 1949. Nylon goods gradually made their way into the shops after the war but remained very scarce.

▽ An extract from a mail order catalogue of 1943. Wartime shoes were designed for comfort and durability rather than for elegance.

## WARDS SHOES FOR COMFORT

**DUTCH TOE**
A Shoe that will go with any outfit. Made on the Dutch Toe last with good strong leather sole and heel. Sizes: 3, 4, 5, 6, 7.
No. G36/603    Black, trimmed Red
No. G36/604    Brown, trimmed Green
Pair **14'7**
7d. extra for carriage.

**ELABORATE INSTEP TIE**
With special wide fitting lines and distinctive tie front. In Glace Kid with comfortable leather heel. Sizes: 3, 4, 5, 6, 7, 8.
No. G36/455    Black.
No. G36/456    Tan.........Pair **25/-**
7d. extra for carriage.

▽ Many clothes in wartime Britain could only be bought with clothing coupons. Each adult had 48 coupons a year.

*New and flattering* BARGAINS

## FASHIONABLE JACKET STYLE

Keeps you warm on cold days. Collarless style with two attractively stitched pockets. Fastens down front with self covered buttons. Long sleeves. Warm but light. Padded shoulders. Shaped back. In Scarlet. Women's size. (5 Coupons)
No. E26/765    **19'6**

**WARDS FOR EASIEST TERMS**

| Value of Order | Monthly Payment | Value of Order | Monthly Payment |
|---|---|---|---|
| Up to £1 | 3/- | £2/10/- | 7/6 |
| £1/5/- | 4/- | £3 | 9/- |
| £1/10/- | 5/- | £3/10/- | 10/- |
| £1/15/- | 5/6 | £4 | 12/- |

## TAILORED SHIRT STYLE

In a soft and comfortable Fibro material which resembles shantung. Long sleeves. Breast pocket with inverted pleat. Inverted pleat down back. Wear with slacks or skirt. Colour: Shantung. Size: Women's

## SPOTTED FIBRO

Soft and warm is this long sleeved Blouse. Buttons all down front. Yoke across back, and inverted pleat. Colours: Red and Blue Sizes: Women's

# Theatre and cinema

Theatres came back into favour during the war, despite the blackout, when for a time, performances were banned although later theatres were allowed to stay open till 6 pm! Long-running plays included Noel Coward's *Blithe Spirit*.

ENSA (Entertainments National Service Association) was formed to entertain the troops and did splendid work throughout the war, even if it was said to stand for "Every Night Something Awful".

Blackout and boredom brought audiences of 25–30 million to the cinema each week. The escapist films provided by Hollywood were easily the favourite type of movie.

◁ Paul Muni as Willy Loman in a performance of *Death of a Salesman* at the Phoenix Theatre, London in 1949. This play by Arthur Miller is about an ordinary man betrayed by the hollow values which are all he knows.

△ Laurence Olivier as *Henry V*. This film, starring Olivier and also directed by him, was shot in Ireland and released in 1944. At that time it was the most expensive film ever made. It was dedicated to those who led the D-Day attack.

▽ Charlie Chaplin in the film *The Great Dictator* (1940). This "withering satire" on Hitler, came too late to amuse Blitz-torn London.

Charlie Chaplin
The Great DICTATOR

△ Noel Coward in the film *In Which We Serve* which was based on the experiences of Lord Mountbatten. The Ministry of Information opposed it on the grounds that it was bad propaganda and Mountbatten appealed to the King to clear it. It mirrored the class structure of the day and was hailed as the finest of the British war movies.

▽ The Marx Brothers were a family of zany American comedians.

▽ Walt Disney, pioneer of full length colour cartoon movies.

△ *Casablanca* was released shortly before Churchill and Roosevelt met at the Casablanca Conference in 1943.

# Sport

During the war years very little sport took place in Britain owing to the call-up of players, the mood of the nation and the requisition of sports grounds for other purposes. The Oval, for instance, became a prisoner of war camp for the duration of the war.

After the war, football had its highest attendances ever and cricket made a similar recovery, though most of the glory went to the Australians.

The Americans proved supreme in tennis and at the 1948 Olympics. Of the minor sports, greyhound racing and speedway proved to be very popular.

△ The 1948 Olympic games held in London and known as the "austerity Olympics" were the first to be held since Hitler's 1936 Nazi propaganda spectacular in Berlin.

▷ Medals struck for the 1948 Olympics were made from oxydised silver instead of the customary gold.

△ Fanny Blankers-Koen, the "Flying Dutchwoman" won 4 medals all for track events, although she was also the world record holder for the high jump.

◁ Stanley Matthews, the "Wizard of Dribble", here in the strip of Stoke City, amazed football crowds with his skills.

▷ Test matches against Australia resumed in 1948. Here the great Don Bradman scores yet another four at the Oval. He retired in 1949 to the sorrow and relief of English cricket fans.

◁ Henry Cotton driving off from the second tee on the Hoylake course during the qualifying round of the British Open Golf Championship in 1947. He won it for the third time in the following year.

▽ Joe Louis, the "Brown Bomber" preparing for his fight against Jersey Joe Walcott. Louis successfully defended his World Heavyweight title 25 times.

◁ Louise Brough playing in the Wimbledon ladies singles final in 1949. She won the title for the third successive time and then for a fourth time in 1955.

# Popular pastimes

World War II was the first war of the radio era and listening to the "wireless" became a national pastime. In between government pep talks encouraging people to save kitchen scraps and waste paper, there were programmes of comedy, such as ITMA (Its That Man Again), and music, such as *Sincerely Yours* with Vera Lynn.

Music and dancing were very popular. Although few songs of any great merit were composed. British songs were often unrelentingly cheerful – as in *Roll Out the Barrel* – or very sentimental – such as *The White Cliffs of Dover*. In fact the most popular song of the war, *Lili Marlene*, was German.

After the war seaside holiday resorts boomed and for those at home, television services resumed for the few who could afford a set.

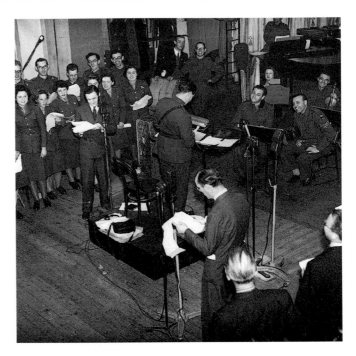

△ Broadcasting to the services. The BBC introduced a special Forces Programme with sport, variety, dance music and news bulletins. This came about partly because the old Home Service was thought to be so boring by the listeners that they preferred to listen to French or German stations!

◁ Open air concerts provided welcome relief for the troops at the front.

◁ (Inset) Vera Lynn, the "Forces Sweetheart". She received a thousand requests a week to sing favourites like *We'll meet again* on the radio. Amazingly the War Office and BBC thought the sentimental lyrics would sap the men's fighting spirit.

△ The *Jitterbug* arrived from America in 1942 and became an immediate craze. Energetic dancing was a great outlet for frayed nerves and boredom.

▽ Holiday resorts were closed during the war and the beaches covered with defences. However, once the mines and wire were cleared after 1945, it was business as usual.

△ The great Glenn Miller. He spent six months in Britain giving concerts before he was lost in a plane crash in 1944. His tune *In the Mood* was one of the best-loved of the war years.

△ An ATS band (top) in full swing. Each service had its own bands. The RAF *Squadronaires* were the best known, but the Army had its *Blue Rockets* and the Navy its *Blue Mariners.*

# The arts

CEMA (Council for the Encouragement of Music and the Arts), a sort of highbrow version of ENSA, was set up to encourage the arts during the war. It employed artists like Nash, Piper, Sutherland and Moore to record the drama of war in their own ways. CEMA also sponsored theatre and ballet tours by the Old Vic and Sadler's Wells' companies to areas outside London.

Classical music was also much in demand. Provincial tours by the London Philharmonic Orchestra proved so popular that extra concerts had to be put on at lunchtimes. Leading orchestras performed concerts for war workers and troops which were always well received. Classical music has probably never been so popular.

After the war CEMA became known as the Arts Council. New provincial theatres were built and some large towns like Bournemouth and Birmingham even started their own orchestras. In this way the arts developed outside of London which had, until now, been their traditional base, and now spread throughout the country.

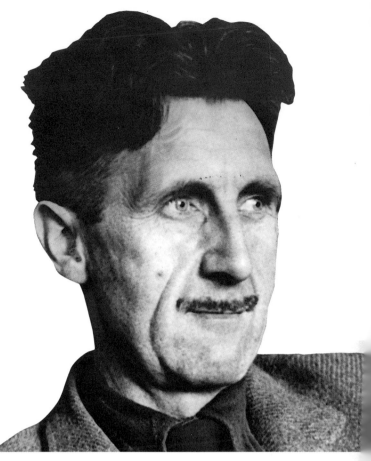

▽ Author Ernest Hemingway used his experiences as a war correspondent to provide vivid backgrounds for his stories.

△ T.S. Eliot (centre), a much honoured poet and playwright. Like Hemingway he won a Nobel prize for literature.

◁ George Orwell, author of *1984* and *Animal Farm*. His books contain powerful social comments which were not usually well received at the time.

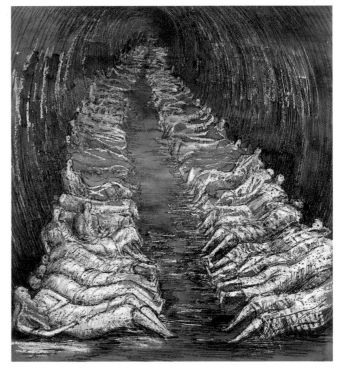

▽ *The Dead Sea* by Paul Nash. As a war artist he used his surrealistic style to produce haunting pictures. This one is part of a group which records the Battle of Britain.

▷ Pen drawing by Henry Moore, *Tube shelter perspective*. Moore was a war artist for two years, and he was also probably the most important 20th century sculptor.

▽ Benjamin Britten working on his opera *Peter Grimes*. His many pieces for children included *The Young Person's Guide to the Orchestra*.

▷ Moira Shearer putting on the red shoes she wore in the film of the same name. It won an Oscar in the 1949 American Academy awards.

# Towards a better world

By the late 1940s there seemed to be every reason to be optimistic about the future. In spite of the hostility between East and West, the world was making a good recovery. Generous aid from the United States helped Europe to avoid some of the worst effects of the post-war period.

In fact by the end of 1946 almost every country had recovered its pre-war economic level. There were still shortages of some goods but wages were generally rising and food prices were low.

There was also a new spirit of international co-operation. The EEC, (European Economic Community), gave Europe another chance of prosperity. The founding of the United Nations offered new hope for a brotherhood of humanity.

△ The 12 member nations signing the Atlantic Treaty in Washington DC in 1949. NATO (the North Atlantic Treaty Organisation) was set up to protect Europe from the new "Red Menace" in Eastern Europe.

◁ The first cargo of American aid under the Marshall Plan reaches Britain. The Minister of Food, John Strachey, watches the unloading with the ship's captain.

▷ The opening session of the United Nations assembly in the Palais de Chaillot, Paris, in 1948. It was hoped that the UN would help nations to solve their disputes peacefully in future. The UN also set up many agencies, such as UNICEF and other relief organisations which distributed money, food and medical supplies to war-stricken countries.

42

▷ Unlike the situation in Britain, the American way of life seemed almost untouched by the effects of the war. In 1945, America was left as the only rich country. It was largely the wealth and generosity of the United States which enabled the world to recover as quickly as it did.

△ The caption reads "With the Marshall Plan inter-European co-operation for a higher standard of living". The Marshall Plan provided over $13 billion to help Europe to recover from the effects of the war. Stalin refused the aid and believed the Plan to be an American attempt to dominate Europe. Well-organised post war relief programmes prevented famine, epidemics and catastrophic upheavals.

▷ The window dresser in Gamages department store hurries to show that certain items of clothing have come off the ration in January 1949. Rationing did not end altogether in Britain until 1953.

# Personalities of the 1940s

**Attlee, Clement** (1883–1967), Prime Minister, 1945–51, of post-war Labour Government, which nationalized coal, railways, gas, electricity and founded the National Health Service.

**Bevan, Aneurin** (1897–1960), Welsh Labour politician who, as Minister of Health 1945–51, pioneered the National Health Service.

**Beveridge, William** (1879–1963), British economist whose survey of social security, the Beveridge Report 1942, led to the founding of the National Health Service after the Second World War.

**Bevin, Ernest** (1881–1951), British Foreign Secretary, in the Labour Government of 1945–51 who welcomed the Marshall Plan and formation of NATO, but became hostile towards Russia and the new state of Israel.

**Britten, Benjamin** (1913–76), an outstanding British pianist, conductor and composer. Among his many works the opera *Peter Grimes* is perhaps the most famous.

**Chaplin, Sir Charles** (1889–1977), known as Charlie. English film actor and director, considered by many to be the greatest star of silent movies. Best known for his slapstick comedy routines.

**Chiang Kai-Shek** (1887–1975), Chinese General and one of the "Big Four" war leaders. Defeated by the Communists, (1949), he retreated from the mainland and founded "National" China on the island of Formosa (Taiwan).

**Churchill, Winston** (1874–1965), As Prime Minister and Minister of Defence from 1940 to 1945, he led and inspired the British people from Dunkirk to the surrender of Germany. His government was defeated by Labour in the 1945 election, but he was again Prime Minister from 1951–1955.

**Crosby, Bing** (1904–77), American crooner, nicknamed the "Old Groaner", whose melodious voice made him the most popular singer of all time.

**Eisenhower, Dwight** (1890–1969), American general, Supreme Commander of Allied Forces in Europe 1944–45. Blessed with inexhaustible patience and tact, "Ike" also possessed the priceless gift of being able to get Allied commanders to work together for victory. In 1953, he became President of the United States.

**Eliot, Thomas Stearns** (1888–1965), American poet, critic and playwright. He became a British subject in 1927. His most famous plays included *Murder in the*

*Cathedral* and *The Family Reunion*. *Old Possum's Book of Practical Cats* has become a classic verse collection.

**Goering, Herman** (1893–1946) A leading Nazi, this former fighter ace, commanded the German *Luftwaffe* throughout World War II, although his greed and laziness made him increasingly unpopular. Sentenced to death for war crimes, he took poison in his cell at Nuremburg.

**Hitler, Adolf** (1889–1945), Austrian megalomaniac who founded the German Nazi party and became Fuhrer of Germany. From 1939 to 1941, his armies overran most of Europe; he then attacked Russia, almost achieving total victory. However, the tide turned against him in 1942 after which there were only major defeats and stubborn retreat. Hitler killed himself amid the ruins of Berlin.

**Mao Tse Tung** (1893–1976), Chinese Communist leader who organised resistance to the Japanese from his headquarters at Yenan in northern China. He drove Chiang Kai-Shek and the Nationalists out of China and became party chairman of the new People's Republic of China in 1949.

**MacArthur, Douglas** (1880–1964), American general, whose "island-hopping" strategy recovered nearly all the Pacific bases captured by the

Clement Attlee

Winston Churchill

Adolf Hitler

Japanese. He commanded the occupation forces in Japan from 1945 until 1951.

**Marshall, George** (1880–1959), American Chief of Staff responsible for planning US military operations throughout the war. As Secretary of State, he initiated the *Marshall Plan* (1948) to help Europe recover. He also helped to create NATO.

**Montgomery, Sir Bernard** (1887–1976), British general, commander of the 8th Army, the Allied forces at Normandy, and the 21st Army Group which he led to victory in Germany. Renowned for being "difficult", he gave his soldiers and the British people what they most wanted – a popular hero who won battles!

**Mountbatten, Louis** (1900–79), British admiral, chief of Combined Operations 1942, Supreme Allied Commander South East Asia 1943–45.

**Mussolini, Benito** (1883–1945), Italian dictator and Hitler's closest ally, until the feeble performance of Italy's forces reduced him to a mere lackey. He was shot by his own countrymen when attempting to flee to Switzerland.

**Nehru, Pandit Jawaharlal** (1889–1964), Prime Minister of India, 1947–64. In spite of years in prison for opposing British rule, Nehru was a strong supporter of the Commonwealth. For India, he worked to improve industry, farming and social welfare.

**Rodgers, Richard** (1902–79), American songwriter. He worked with Lorenz Hart and Oscar Hammerstein to produce some of the best-loved musicals ever written.

**Rommel, Erwin** (1891–1944), German general and master of desert warfare whom Montgomery defeated at El Alamein. Rommel commanded the German forces which opposed the Allied invasion of Normandy. He committed suicide after the failure of a German army plot to assassinate Hitler.

**Roosevelt, Franklin Delano** (1882–1945), President of the United States 1933–45. Before Pearl Harbour, he supported the Allied cause and formed a close understanding with Churchill and, later, with Stalin. His mistakes have been much criticised, but by his actions he saved Britain and much of Europe from the horrors of Nazi domination.

**Sinatra, Frank** (1915-1998), American singer, actor, composer, who reached stardom in the 1940s: the first of the pop-idols to rouse his fans to screaming pitch.

**Stalin, Josef** (1879–1953), Russian leader, from 1924 to 1953, who joined Hitler in crushing Poland and then accepted Allied aid after Germans attacked Russia. He never relaxed his hostility to the West, and made it his policy to bring the whole of eastern Europe under Soviet control.

**Tito, Josip Broz (Marshall)** (1892–1980), President of Yugoslavia, who led the partisans so well against the occupying Germans that he was able to form a Communist government after the war and even to defy Stalin.

**Tojo, Hideki** (1884-1948), Japanese general and Prime Minister who urged close collaboration with Germany and authorized the attack on Pearl Harbor. After the war he was hanged for major war crimes.

**Truman, Harry** (1884–1972), American President, 1945–53, who succeeded Roosevelt and made the decision to use atomic bombs against Japan. Later the "Truman Doctrine" promised American aid to any free nation resisting Communist pressure.

**Zhukov, Georgi** (1896–1974), Russian general who successfully defended Leningrad and Moscow against the German offensives, planned victory at Stalingrad and the fall of Berlin in 1945.

**Field-Marshall Montgomery**

**Franklin D. Roosevelt**

**Josef Stalin**

# 1940s year by year

## 1940

- Germany invades Denmark and Norway.
- Churchill becomes Prime Minister.
- German armies invade Holland, Belgium and France.
- British army evacuated from Dunkirk.
- Germans take Paris.
- Italy enters the war.
- France capitulates.
- Battle of Britain: the RAF defeats the Luftwaffe.
- The German-Italian-Japanese Pact.
- Food rationing starts in Britain.
- Roosevelt re-elected President.
- Home Guard formed in Britain.
- Sikorsky helicopter flies in the United States.
- Duke Ellington plays jazz.

## 1941

- Roosevelt signs Lease Lend Act.
- Germans overrun Yugoslavia, Greece and Crete.
- Malta bombed.
- German battleship *Bismarck* sunk.
- Germans invade Russia and reach the outskirts of Leningrad and Moscow.
- Churchill and Roosevelt meet to sign the Atlantic Charter.
- Japanese planes bomb Pearl Harbour.
- Japan attacks the Philippines.
- Germany and Italy declare war on the United States of America.
- Clothes rationing starts in Britain.
- Britain tests the first jet-fighter, the *Gloster*.
- Commercial television begins in the United States.
- Japanese capture Guam, Wake Island and Hong Kong.
- Noel Coward produces *Blithe Spirit*.

## 1942

- Japanese invade Burma, Malaya, the Dutch East Indies and capture Rangoon, Singapore and Bataan.
- Rommel captures Tobruk in North Africa.
- US Navy wins vital battles of the Coral Sea and Midway Island.
- Germans surrounded at Stalingrad.
- Montgomery's 8th Army defeats Rommel at El Alamein. Rommel retreats.
- American and British troops land in French North Africa.
- US marines take Guadalcanal. MacArthur begins "island hopping".
- British and Indian troops invade Burma.
- Gandhi demands that the British should "Quit India".
- First electronic computer is built.
- Sugar, coffee and petrol rationed in the United States.
- OXFAM is founded.
- Bing Crosby croons *White Christmas*. Vera Lynn sings *We'll Meet Again*. The troops sing *Lilli Marlene*.
- ITMA cheers up Britain.

## 1943

- Churchill and Roosevelt meet at Casablanca in North Africa.
- Germans surrender at Stalingrad.
- Russians recover city after city as they drive the enemy westwards.
- Allies carry out day and night bombing of Germany.
- RAF bomb Berlin.
- Mussolini overthrown. Italy joins the Allies.
- Roosevelt, Churchill and Stalin meet at Tehran.
- US forces continue island-hopping towards the Philippines.
- *H.M.S. Duke of York* sinks German battlecruiser *Scharnhorst* in Atlantic.
- Penicillin saves many lives.
- *Oklahoma* takes New York by storm.
- Jitterbug dancing is all the rage.

## 1944

- Americans recapture islands in the Pacific.
- D-Day landings in Normandy.
- July Plot by Army officers fails to kill Hitler.
- Polish uprising in Warsaw crushed by the Germans.
- Allies invade southern France.
- Allies enter Paris, Brussels and Antwerp.
- V2 rockets bombard London.
- Allied advance checked by German successes at Arnhem and in the Ardennes.
- British troops enter Athens.
- US troops invade Philippines.
- Japanese navy decisively beaten in the battle of the Leyte Gulf.
- Ho Chi Minh declares Vietnam's independence from France.
- Blackout is relaxed in Britain.
- Olivier's film *Henry V* released.

## 1945

- Churchill, Roosevelt and Stalin meet at Yalta.
- US troops capture Manila and Okinawa, only 560 km (350 miles) from Japan.
- Allied forces cross the river Rhine into Germany.
- Mussolini killed by Italian partisans.
- Hitler commits suicide.
- British forces recapture Rangoon.
- Roosevelt dies and is succeeded by Harry Truman.
- Germany surrenders.
- Victory in Europe (V.E. day).
- United Nations Charter signed.
- US planes bomb Japan.
- Truman, Stalin and Attlee meet at Potsdam.
- Atomic bomb destroys Hiroshima.
- Japan surrenders.

- World War II ends.
- Civil war breaks out in China.
- Tito becomes head of Yugoslavia.
- Orwell's novel *Animal Farm* published.
- The Atomic Research Centre at Harwell opened.

# 1946

- The first session of the UN General Assembly opens in London. Paul Spaak of Belgium becomes the first president.
- De Gaulle resigns the Presidency of France.
- Germany divided into four occupation zones. Berlin divided into four sectors.
- Churchill makes his Iron Curtain speech in Fulton, Missouri.
- Peace Conference held in Paris.
- The United States and Britain merge their occupation zones in Germany.
- Truman approves a loan to Britain.
- Labour government nationalizes the Bank of England, the coal industry and civil aviation.
- The Philippines become independent.
- Bread rationed in Britain.
- US navy explodes underwater atomic bomb at Bikini.
- UNESCO (United Nations Economic and Social Council) founded.
- Electronic brain built in the United States.
- The musical *Annie Get Your Gun* opens in New York.
- London Airport opens.
- Joe Louis wins his 23rd defence of the world heavy-weight title.
- Cinema attendance in Britain reaches an all-time high.

# 1947

- The coldest winter in Britain for 56 years leads to coal shortages and potato rationing.
- Marshall Plan announced to aid European recovery.
- Burma chooses independence.
- India divided into two dominions: India (Hindu) and Pakistan (Muslim).
- British railways, road transport and the electricity industry nationalized.
- Princess Elizabeth marries Lieutenant Philip Mountbatten.
- First nuclear reactor built at Harwell, England.
- "New Look" fashions arrive.
- *Diary of Anne Frank* published.
- American pilot flies the first supersonic plane at 1547 kph (967 mph).
- First "flying saucers" reported.
- School-leaving age raised to 15 in Britain.
- *Kon-Tiki* raft sailed from Peru to Polynesia.

# 1948

- Gandhi assassinated by a Hindu fanatic in India.
- Pakistan leader Jinnah dies.
- Berlin airlift begins.
- Jewish state of Israel proclaimed.
- World Health Organisation founded.
- South Africa adopts apartheid.
- Transistors and long-playing records are invented in the United States.
- National Health Service is set up in Britain.
- The world's first port radar system is in use at Liverpool.
- The Organization of European Economic Co-operation (OEEC), the forerunner of the European Common Market, is founded.
- Rocket missiles tested in the United States.
- North Korea declares itself to be a republic under Kim Il Sung. Hopes of reuniting North and South Korea fade.
- Truman elected President of the United States.

- Henry Cotton wins the British Open golf championship.
- Olivier's film of *Hamlet* released.
- At the Olympic Games which are held in London, the Dutch athlete Fanny Blankers-Koen wins four gold medals.
- Norman Mailer's war novel, *The Naked and the Dead* is published.

# 1949

- Twelve nations sign a treaty setting up the North Atlantic Treaty Organisation (NATO).
- Republic of Ireland leaves the British Commonwealth.
- Indonesia declares her independence.
- France grants independence to Vietnam.
- Adenauer becomes the first Chancellor of the German Federal Republic (West Germany).
- Russia lifts the Berlin blockade and establishes the German Democratic Republic (East Germany) in the Soviet zone.
- Nehru becomes Prime Minster of India.
- Arab-Israeli armistice. Jerusalem is partitioned between Israel and Jordan.
- People's Republic of China proclaimed under Mao Tse Tung. Chiang Kai-Shek sets up Nationalist China on the island of Formosa.
- The Soviet Union tests its first atomic bomb.
- Clothes rationing ends in Britain.
- First jet airliner, the *Comet*, developed.
- The stage musical *South Pacific* opens in New York.
- George Orwell's frightening vision of the future *Nineteen Eighty-four* published.
- The film *The Third Man* released.

# Index